WRITTEN BY
MIKE TUCKER

ILLUSTRATED BY
JONATRONIX

TIME'S PENDULUM

Contents

My name is **Birdy**, and I'm from future Earth. 2099 to be precise. My world is at risk – a giant asteroid is on a collision course with the planet.

Kalvin Spearhead, head of **END CO** – the most powerful company on Earth – plans to build a giant vortex machine to send people back in time to escape the asteroid. He has assembled a team of human-like robots, **Tick-Tock Men**, to collect seven **Artefacts of Time**. These Artefacts will be used to power his machine.

My gran, **Professor Martin**, is the head scientist at END CO. She has shown me Spearhead's plans; she doesn't think his machine is capable of transporting vast numbers of people. Even if the machine does work, it will have a devastating effect on history: it could change everything! Gran has tried to tell Spearhead, but he won't listen. I decided I had to try to stop him. I have borrowed one of my gran's old-tech time-travel vortex machines – an **Escape Wheel** – and am trying to reach the Artefacts of Time before the Tick-Tock Men do.

Luckily, I'm not alone on my journey. I've met four new friends – **Max**, **Cat**, **Ant** and **Tiger**. They have special watches that can make them shrink to micro-size … which comes in handy when the Tick-Tock Men try to stop us!

Chapter 1: The workshop

The attic room was silent and still when, suddenly, the dust in the air began to swirl furiously …

Hmmmmmmmmm!

In a blaze of light, five friends emerged from the vortex … into a new time period.

Is everyone OK?

Where are we?

It looks like an attic.

Are you sure we're in the right place?

Of course … I mean, I'm pretty sure we are.

So, which country are we in?

And what period in history?

We're in the city of The Hague, in the Netherlands. Sixteenth century. Right where we're meant to be.

Hey, come and see.

I was right. It is The Hague.

So, the pendulum clock should be somewhere close by then?

You mean, the very *first* pendulum clock, invented by Christiaan Huygens.

Huygens? Didn't he discover Saturn's rings? And its moon – Titan?

They named a NASA spacecraft after him.

He was a scientist and a mathematician. But he was also interested in clocks.

Well, there aren't any clocks up here.

Wait a moment … I think I can hear ticking!

TICK! TOCK!
TICK! TOCK!

It's coming from downstairs.

TICK! TOCK!
TICK! TOCK!

The Tick-Tock Men must have got here before us!

The readings on my pocket watch show there's been other vortex activity recently.

Listen to that noise. There must be hundreds of them.

TICK! TOCK! TICK! TOCK! TICK! TOCK! TICK! TOCK!

What are we going to do?

We don't have a lot of choice, do we? If the pendulum clock is nearby, then we have to locate it before the Tick-Tock Men do.

You've got the torch, Tiger, so you'd better lead the way.

Great.

Nervously, Tiger led the way down the rickety, wooden staircase.

TICK! TOCK! TICK! TOCK!

Suddenly …

Ssssh!

Creeeeak!

The room must be full of Tick-Tockers!

TICK! TOCK! TICK!
TOCK! TICK! TOCK!
TICK! TOCK! TICK!
TOCK! TICK! TOCK!

Open the door slowly … I'll cover you.

Tiger slowly eased the door open and was confronted by a remarkable sight.

Gasp!

TICK! TOCK!
TICK! TOCK!

The friends were in a clockmaker's workshop.

TICK! TOCK! TICK! TOCK! TICK! TICK! TOCK!

No bad guys – correction, bad *robots* – after all!

TICK! TOCK! TICK! TOCK!

There's still at least one Tick-Tock Man in this time period though. Let's start looking for that pendulum clock!

None of these clocks seem to have a pendulum.

Perhaps we're too early … in history, I mean. Perhaps it's not been built yet.

I think you could be right. These look like the plans for the clock.

Let me see!

These are the ones all right! We must be in the workshop of Salomon Coster!

I thought Huygens was the inventor?

Huygens invented the pendulum clock, but it was Coster who actually built it.

Ant activated the camera on his watch.

Huygens' original plans! I have to get a shot of these.

Put the plans on the floor. I want to get a good angle.

Just hurry up … this isn't a sight-seeing trip.

Ant had only taken a couple of pictures when …

Someone's coming!

It could be the Tick-Tock Men!

Thump! Thump! Thump!

Shrink! Now!

The figure of Salomon Coster loomed in the doorway.

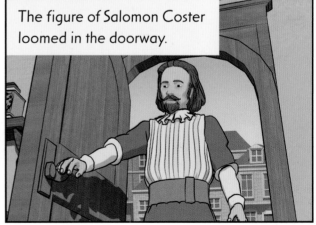

Meanwhile, on top of the workbench …

It was a good thing I was able to grab hold of you before I shrank.

I just wish you'd climbed off the bench before you did! Now what are we going to do?

Now, where was I …? Everything is such a mess in here. I really should tidy up before Mr Huygens arrives.

Get down. He's coming this way!

I don't remember leaving these on the floor. Ah, well … I'd better get started again.

We need a better hiding place. We're way too exposed here!

Where do you suggest?

Hmmm, what next?

There's the shell of a clock over there – we'll aim for that.

He could look round at any moment.

Then we'd better hurry!

Seizing the moment, Birdy dashed forwards towards safety …

… but Ant hesitated.

Come on, Ant!

Here goes nothing!

Whaaaat?

I … I don't believe it!

Uh oh!

The clockmaker reached out with a huge hand. There was no way that Ant could escape.

Ahhh! Let me go!

You can speak?

Remarkable. What manner of creature are you? Where did you come from?

I must make a proper examination of you.

An examination?

You could be the scientific find of the century! I must find my magnifying glass.

Birdy! Get me out of here!

It's no good. I can't move it on my own!

Let's both push together.

Get ready to duck!

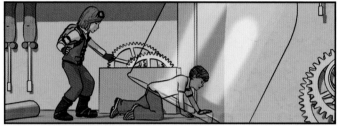

SMAAASH!

The shattering of glass attracted the clockmaker's attention.

No!

He's coming back! This time he'll catch both of us!

But Birdy had other ideas.

Not if I have anything to do with it.

Grab on!

Salomon couldn't believe his eyes.

Two of them! They can even fly, like insects.

Back on the floor ... Max, Cat and Tiger had watched their friends' daring escape.

Birdy!

Down here!

Hurry!

There's no point trying to hide.

So, there's a whole colony of you! I shall be famous!

Knock! Knock!

Salomon?

The door swung open to reveal Christiaan Huygens. He had come to check on the progress of his clock.

What on earth are you doing down there?

Master Huygens!

Thank goodness you're here. I've made the most extraordinary discovery.

Oh? What might that be?

Tiny people, the size of insects. A new species!

Really …

I have the creatures trapped. See for yourself!

It will be the scientific breakthrough of the century.

The evidence that Salomon needed to convince his employer had vanished.

Whaaat?

Your jest is not appreciated, Master Coster.

I do not understand …

We moved just in time!

If you hadn't spotted this mouse hole in the skirting board, Tiger …

I came here to observe your progress on my clock. Instead I find that the work is yet to commence, and you're wasting your time with fantasies!

I promise you, sir, I did not imagine these things! See the remains of the glass under which I trapped one of them.

It is clear to me that you are just wasting time!

Sir, please …

Enough!

I was led to believe that you were a skilled clockmaker —

I am. I beseech you …

You have one last chance, Master Coster. Prove to me that I was not mistaken in giving you the job of making my clock, or I will take the work elsewhere.

I shall return later to check on your progress.

SLAAAM!

Salomon Coster backed nervously away.

TICK! TOCK!

TICK! TOCK!

Who on earth are you?

FZAAAAT!

Plans acquired. Escape Wheel energy low. Will recharge then return to base.

We've got to stop him. Get me back to full size!

Hold it right there!

BLAMMM!

FZAAAAT!

The energy beam from the Tick-Tock Man's Time Paralysis Weapon split the room …

FZAAAAT!

Look out!

When the friends got to their feet, the Tick-Tock Man had gone.

Ant leant on the workbench …

Hey!

Your hand went right through it!

What's happening to me?

It's not just you.

We're all fading!

Oh no …

There was always a danger that this could occur.

That *what* could occur?

Everything that we do in the past affects the future. In this time, in this place, Salomon Coster is meant to build the clock for Huygens. Now that the Tick-Tock Man has stolen those plans, he can't do that.

So because that clock doesn't get built, the future has been altered.

But why is that affecting us?

Because one little change in the past might cause a big change in the future. You four might never have met; your watches might not have been invented …

… We might not even have been born!

So, what are you saying, that we are going to vanish from existence completely?

Maybe. Until things are decided here for certain we will continue to fade in and out of reality.

But while we're still here, there's a chance that we can put things right.

Hey, I'm becoming solid again!

The effect will come and go until history has settled.

Then we need to get after that Tick-Tock Man before he takes those plans back to the future … and back to Spearhead.

We can't just leave Salomon paralyzed like this. Someone might find him.

We need to split up. Cat, Tiger, you come with me. We'll go after the Tick-Tock Man.

What about me?

You try and unfreeze Salomon. And just in case we don't get those plans back … Ant, you get busy redrawing them.

Me?

You've got photos of the plans on your watch, remember!

Oh. Ok.

We'd better get going. It looks like there's a storm building. We need to find the Tick-Tock Man before he can harness enough energy to recharge his Escape Wheel.

You might need this.

Thanks.

Where do we start looking?

I'll try and track the Tick-Tock Man's energy on my watch.

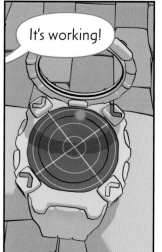

It's working!

The tracking signal led them down a narrow alleyway.

There he is!

What's he just standing there for?

Perhaps he's waiting for the lightning.

I just hope he stays still while I aim this thing.

Uh oh! He heard you!

Quick, Cat. Fire!

BLAAM!

WHOOSH!

It went right through him!

He's fading in and out of time just like us.

Look out!

Don't worry. He can't get us if he's insubstantial.

BLAAAM!

Aaaah!

Of course he can still get us.

But only when he's solid. Right?

Solid once more, the Tick-Tock Man picked up his Escape Wheel and retreated.

After him!

Escape Wheels are devices that allow people to travel through time by creating a time vortex. Wheels require a large amount of energy to get the vortex to work, such as a lightning bolt from a storm. The further you want to jump back or forward in time, the more energy the wheels require. They need to be recharged every now and then. Running low on energy during a time jump can be extremely dangerous and can lead to pit-stopping – when you have to jump out of the vortex as soon as possible. This is dangerous because you never know where or when you're going to end up. If the wheel's energy fails completely mid-jump, then the vortex could collapse in on itself, trapping the jumper inside, or worse, crushing them into oblivion.

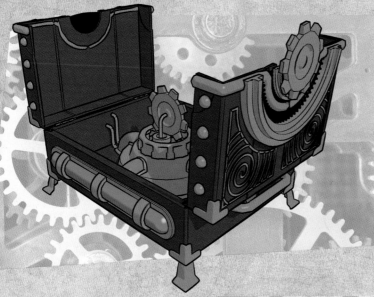

Birdy's Escape Wheel is considered to be 'old-tech' where she comes from. It doesn't always work that well, which was how she ended up meeting Max, Cat, Ant and Tiger – by pit-stopping in their time.

Tick-Tock Men have more advanced wheels that can pinpoint their destination, time and location with more accuracy. Their enhanced functionality, however, means that they require even more energy to work properly and regularly need recharging.

Chapter 4: Fading hope

Meanwhile, back at Salomon Coster's workshop …

Isn't that your Escape Wheel?

Yes.

I'm going to try to use the vortex energy to unfreeze Salomon.

How are you getting on with redrawing those plans?

It's hard as I keep fading!

I'm better at making things than drawing them, anyway.

Meanwhile ... Max, Cat and Tiger were still on the trail of the Tick-Tock Man, and the storm was building.

Did anyone see where he went? My watch is playing up. I've lost him.

He could be anywhere!

He'll be trying to get to somewhere high. Somewhere lightning is more likely to strike.

DONG! ... DONG! ... DONG! ...

Like a bell tower, you mean?

It's worth a try. Let's go ...

Why didn't I get Birdy's Caliber Glove?

Never mind that, Tiger. Just run!

I can't see him!

Just then ...

Cat!

FZAAT!

Chapter 5: Pigeon plan

Back in the workshop, Birdy glanced over at the bench …

I'm impressed.

Thanks. How are you getting on?

All done!

Well, what are you waiting for? Let's unfreeze Salomon!

No, wait a minute.

I don't understand. If the machine is finished, then why not use it?

You've made a good start on the clock.

Yes, but …

Then why stop now? Finish the job and *then* we'll wake him up. That way we'll be certain to get history back on track!

I don't know. There's a lot still left to do …

You need to have more confidence in yourself, Ant. I know you can do it. Come on, I'll help.

Meanwhile, in the square ...

What do we do now? Go after the Tick-Tock Man?

We can't leave Cat here on her own. We'll just have to wait until she unfreezes.

But that could take hours!

Suddenly Cat groaned, and started to move her fingers.

Hey, look!

The fading must have affected the way that the Time Paralysis Weapon works.

Ooooh, my head.

BAROOOOM!

The Tick-Tock Man must be at the top by now...

... Waiting for the lightning.

We've got to get up there and stop him before he has enough power to time jump.

A minute later …

Right, Tiger. See if you can get close to them.

Perhaps you can tempt them over. Got any food?

I think I have a biscuit. Do pigeons like biscuits?

Here, birdy. Nice birdy.

Now, Max!

Good luck!

Yes! I was right – they're taking us straight to the tower. It must be where they roost.

Now it's up to Tiger to create that distraction.

There's the Tick-Tock Man.

TICK! TOCK! TICK! TOCK!

Looks like he's got his Escape Wheel ready!

Now all he needs is the lightning.

As if on cue, a flash of lightning lit up the sky.

Can you shut him down?

I don't know if the Caliber Glove is going to work on him whilst we're micro-size.

If we grow to normal size, he's bound to see us.

Then Tiger had better hurry up with that distraction.

I hope that the others have made it to the top safely.

There he is!

Hey! Clockwork brain! Over here!

FZAAAT!

Wooah!

That was close!

Max and Cat seized their chance.

Now, Cat!

Hurry!

I'm trying. It's jammed or something.

Stupid glove!

Move!

Max and Cat dived out of the way just as the Tick-Tock Man fired.

Interfering human!

Uh oh!

BLAMM!

At last!

Cat hit the robot in the back of the neck, forcing him to wind down.

Winding d ... o ... w ... n.

Good riddance!

VSSSSSIPPT!

Back at Salomon Coster's workshop …

There! It's finished.

I knew you could do it!

You're back!

Did you manage to deal with the Tick-Tock Man?

Yes, and we got the plans back!

So all that work on the clock was for nothing!

Not exactly, Ant. Huygens is coming back …

Time to get Salomon unfrozen. You others had better hide.

He's going to get such a surprise when he wakes up and realizes that the clock has been finished for him.

BZZZZZ!

Nearly there!

Slowly, Salomon started to move once more.

Hmm … What? I must have fallen asleep.

I suppose I'd better get on with that clock …

But what's this …?

How?

Well, Master Coster, have you finished? The clock tower bells did not chime correctly today, so I fear that this city is in great need of a reliable clock!

It's here.

This is most splendid! You are indeed as good a craftsman as I had been told!

He's never going to know what really happened.

Good. The less impact we have on history the better.

So, where do we go next?

It looks like we need to go forward in time. But the readings are strange. The coordinates look as though they are moving.

Let's just hope we can get there before the Tick-Tock Men.

Yes, I don't fancy fading again.

Well, there's no point in hanging around here. Everybody ready?

Birdy set the coordinates on her Escape Wheel … ready for another adventure.

Christiaan Huygens was born in The Hague, in the Netherlands, in 1629. His father was a famous statesman, scientist, poet and musician. However, Christiaan would go on to be even more famous than his dad! He studied hard and became a mathematician, physicist and an astronomer.

Christiaan had many great achievements in his life, including formulating the wave theory of light, discovering Saturn's rings and one of its moons, and, of course, inventing the pendulum clock.

The pendulum clock was significant because it was far more reliable than any previous mechanical timepiece. The pendulum clock remained the most accurate type of clock in the world for the next 300 years, although many improvements were made to Christiaan Huygens' design during that period.

Christiaan died on 8th July, 1695, aged 66.